POCKET QUIZ

Alle Pocket-Quiz im Überblick

W0391329

Ab Frühjahr 2008 außerdem erhältlich:

Pocket Quiz

- Kopftraining
- Klassiker der Weltliteratur
- Jazz
- Olympia
- Flugzeuge
- Kultserien

Erhältlich im gut sortierten Buchhandel und bei:

moses.

moses. Verlag GmbH • Arnoldstraße 13d
D-47906 Kempen • www.moses-verlag.de

Question

1. Make two present tense sentences.
stock market - over-valued. - Specialists - expect - correction - soon.

2. Put in the fitting word: *fabrication, factory* or *fabric*?

They have a ... for car components in the Czech Republic.

3. Match up the sentences.
You hand in receipts
in a cookery book.
You get a prescription
with your tax return.
You find recipes
from your doctor.

Answer

1. The stock market is over-valued. Specialists expect a correction soon.
2. They have a factory for car components in the Czech Republic.
3. You hand in receipts with your tax return. You get a prescription from your doctor. You find recipes in a cookery book.

business vocabulary:

tax return – Steuererklärung

Question

1. What do these abbreviations stand for?
   - incl.
   - PTO

2. Put in *Re: / In reference to / Referring.*
   ... your letter dated 4/6/02, we can inform you of the following.
   ... Your letter dated 4/6/02.
   ... to your letter of 4/6/02, we can inform you of the following.
3. Which phrase fits?
   We *are happy / look forward* to a good working relationship with your company.

Answer

1. • including
   • please turn over (dt. bitte wenden)
2. In reference to your letter dated 4/6/02, we can inform you of the following.
   Re: Your letter dated 4/6/02.
   Referring to your letter of 4/6/02, we can inform you of the following.
3. We look forward to a good working relationship with your company.

Question

1. Choose the right word.
   The *personal / personell* manager is arranging an interview with Helen, who has applied for a job as an office manager's *personal / personell* assistant.
2. Being polite. Which of the sentences sounds wrong?
   - Thank you for sparing me your valuable time.
   - I don't want to spoil your precious time.
   - I'm grateful you found time to see me.

3. Can you get the word order right?
   First – last week – some of the points – to recapitulate – we discussed on the phone – I would like

Answer

1. The personell manager is arranging an interview with Helen, who has applied for a job as an office manager's personal assistant.
2. I don't want to spoil your precious time.

3. First I would like to recapitulate some of the points we discussed on the phone last week.

Question

1. A recorded message. Choose the fitting phrases.
   I'm afraid no one's *available / unable* to take your call at the moment, but if you'd like to *leave / withdraw* your name and number, we'll call you *back / recall* you as soon as possible. Please *talk / speak* after the tone.

2. Say the telephone number *6887000*.
3. Complete the dialogue.
   This is - calling back - can I do - a message
   "... Kenneth James. I got ... to call you."
   "Good morning, Ken. Thanks for ... ."
   "What ... for you?"

Answer

1. I'm afraid no one's available to take your call at the moment, but if you'd like to leave your name and number, we'll call you back as soon as possible. Please speak after the tone.
2. six double eight seven oh double oh

3. "This is Kenneth James. I got a message to call you."
"Good morning, Ken. Thanks for calling back."
"What can I do for you?"

Question

1. *if* or *that*?
   She's sure ... the teddy bears are being delivered tomorrow morning.
   I doubt ... they really are.

2. "Mr. Jones had a car accident last week."
   Which response doesn't fit?
   - "Oh dear!"
   - "I'm impressed."

3. Present your company.
   set up – employs – Germany's biggest – major – headquarters – high quality
   German Toys is ... mail-order house for ... toys. The company ... 250 people, 150 of whom work in the Berlin ... . The others run our shops, which have been ... in all ... German cities.

Answer

1. She's sure that the teddy bears are being delivered tomorrow morning.
   I doubt if they really are.
2. "I'm impressed."

3. German Toys is Germany's biggest mail-order house for high quality toys. The company employs 250 people, 150 of whom work in the Berlin headquarters. The others run our shops, which have been set up in all major German cities.

business vocabulary:
to set up – gründen

Question

1. Match the verbs with the prepositions.

to account	with
to distribute	for
to supply	to

2. *tender, quotation* or *offer*?
His ... for my car was ridiculous.
They handed in the lowest ... for the electrical equipment of the new school building.
Please send us your ... for 25 robot dogs.

3. Can you get the word order right?
this offer – to refer to – please do not forget – If you accept – quotation No. 123

Answer

1. account for
   to distribute to
   to supply with

2. His offer for my car was ridiculous.
   They handed in the lowest tender for the electrical equipment of the new school building. Please send us your quotation for 25 robot dogs.

3. If you accept this offer please do not forget to refer to quotation No. 123.

business vocabulary:

tender – Ausschreibungsangebot
quotation – Preisangabe, Angebot

Question

1. The recruitment process. Match up the phrases.

to advertise	for an interview
to check	a vacancy
to invite s.o.	the references

2. *in* or *from*?
   Experience ... the trade is a must. We also expect you to type documents ... dictation and compose letters ... notes.

3. Which adjective fits? A person ...
   ... who can adapt to changing circumstances is *flexible / logical*.
   ... who has two mother tongues is *literate / bilingual*.
   ... who is able to make decisions is *decisive / persuasive*.

Answer

1. to advertise a vacancy
   to check the references
   to invite s.o. for an interview

2. Experience in the trade is a must. We also expect you to type documents from dictation and compose letters from notes.

3. A person ...
   ... who can adapt to changing circumstances is flexible.
   ... who has two mother tongues is bilingual.
   ... who is able to make decisions is decisive.

Question

1. Can you match up the phrases?

to write	a business
to run	cash
to pay	out a checque

2. Choose the fitting verb.
   They were hit so badly by the recession they had to *borrow / lend* money.
   The bank, however, refused to *lend / borrow* them any more.

3. Complete the sentences using *are getting* ...!
   Computers and software ... (continually / cheap).
   Cars ... (still / expensive).

Answer

1. to write out a checque
   to run a business
   to pay cash

2. They were hit so badly by the recession they had to borrow money.
   The bank, however, refused to lend them any more.

3. Computers and software are continually getting cheaper.
   Cars are still getting more expensive.

Question

1. Book a flight to London: business class, December 2nd.
2. Departure. Complete the following announcements.
   proceed – boarding card – passengers – departure – for boarding
   Lufthansa announce the ... of Flight No. 101 to Berlin. Will all ... for this flight please ... to Gate 2.
   Flight No. 101 is now ready ... . Please have your ... ready.
3. What are these cities called in English?
   Brüssel • Moskau • Köln • Neapel • München • Mailand

Answer

1. I would like to book a business class flight to London on December 2nd, please.
2. departure – passengers – proceed – for boarding – boarding card
3. Brussels • Moscow • Cologne • Naples • Munich • Milan

Question

1. "Do you mind if I smoke?"
Which answer doesn't fit?
   - "No, not at all."
   - "Yes, please."
   - "I'm afraid this is a non-smoking area."

2. Can you match up the phrases?

on	morning
in the	lunchtime
at	Tuesday

3. Present simple or present continuous?
She ... from France but at the moment she ... in Germany. (to come, to live)
I usually ... till five, but today I ... late. (to work, to stay)

Answer

1. "Yes, please."
2. in the morning
   at lunchtime
   on Tuesday

3. She comes from France but at the moment she is living in Germany.
   I usually work till five, but today I am staying late.

Question

1. Can you get the word order right?
that we will only be – to our offer dated October 15th – Since you have – we would like to point out – in a position to deliver – until December 15th – not yet reacted – according to the terms quoted

2. Put in the fitting forms of *to take* and *to allow*.
Your offer can only ... into consideration if we ... a quantity rebate of 15 %.

3. Match up the sentences.

We are placing	withdraw our offer.
We are forced	the following order.
Hereby we	to cancel our order.

Answer

1. Since you have not yet reacted to our offer dated October 15th we would like to point out that we will only be in a position to deliver according to the terms quoted until December 15th.

2. Your offer can only be taken into consideration if we are allowed a quantity rebate of 15 %.

3. We are placing the following order.
We are forced to cancel our order.
Hereby we withdraw our offer.

Question

1. *take-over, merger* or *joint-venture*?
When two companies co-operate in a certain project, it's called a ... .
When two companies are combined into one, this is a ... .
When one company takes control of another, it's called a ... .

2. Can you match up the phrases?

suitable	of
satisfied	for
proud	with

3. Complete the sentences using *to commission* and *to reach.*
Unfortunately we could not ... an agreement.
Before we decide we have to ... an expert opinion.

Answer

1. When two companies cooperate in a certain project, it's called a joint-venture. When two companies are combined into one, this is a merger. When one company takes control of another, it's called a take-over.
2. suitable for (auch: suitable to)
   satisfied with
   proud of
3. Unfortunately we could not reach an agreement. Before we decide we have to commission an expert opinion.

business vocabulary:

to commission – in Auftrag geben
expert opinion – Expertise
merger – Fusion

Question

1. Make a dialogue.
   - Wilson Electronics, Chicago - What - do - for you?
   - Helmut Roth - Computer Maier, Munich. - put me through - to Mr. James?
   - trying - connect you. - afraid - he - on the other line. - leave - message for him?
2. Say the telephone number *4531099*.
3. Can you help Ulrike Maurer to leave a recorded message? She wants to be called back. It's urgent. Her number is 07777 / 50011.

Answer

1. "Wilson Electronics, Chicago. What can I do for you?"
   "This is Helmut Roth from Computer Maier, Munich. Could you please put me through to Mr. James?"
   "Trying to connect you. I'm afraid he's on the other line. Would you like to leave a message for him?"

2. four five three one oh double nine
3. Hello, this is Ulrike Maurer. Could you call me back as soon as possible, please? It's urgent. My number is 07777/50011.

Question

1. Introduce yourself and your colleagues.
   introduce – this is – from Berlin – to meet you – introduce myself
   "Excuse me, may I ... ? I'm Sandra Maier ... ."
   "I'm Michael Butler. Ms. Maier, may I ... Ms. Watkins, our advertising manager. Ms. Watkins, ... Ms. Maier."
   "Pleased ... ."
2. "The meeting is at half three."

   Is it at  or at  ?

3. Someone says: "Thank you very much." Which response doesn't fit?
   - "You're welcome."
   - "My pleasure."
   - "Never mind."

Answer

1. "Excuse me, may I introduce myself? I'm Sandra Maier from Berlin."

   "I'm Michael Butler. Ms. Maier, may I introduce Ms. Watkins, our advertising manager. Ms. Watkins, this is Ms. Maier."
   "Pleased to meet you."

2. It's at

3. "Never mind."

Question

1. Complete the following part of an offer.
   to guarantee them – quoted prices – our terms of business – of our talking dolls – the minimum order
   For the items offered above ... amounts to 70 pieces. The ... include packing, insurance and freight. The quality ... makes it possible for us ... for 2 years. Enclosed please find ... .

2. Choose the fitting words.
   Please inform us if you are in *attachment* / *agreement* with these terms.
   The prices are *valid* / *solid* only until 2/12/97.
3. *with* or *in*?
   to agree ...
   to invest ...

Answer

1. For the items offered above the minimum order amounts to 70 pieces. The quoted prices include packing, insurance and freight. The quality of our talking dolls makes it possible for us to guarantee them for 2 years. Enclosed please find our terms of business.

2. Please inform us if you are in agreement with these terms.
   The prices are valid only until 2/12/97.

3. to agree with
   to invest in

Question

1. At the trade fair. Can you match up the phrases?

application	rental
catalogue	deadline
stand	of exhibitors

2. Complete the sentences.
do you need – press release – complimentary tickets – list us
Please ... in the catalogue of exhibitors.
How many ... can we have?
When ... the promotional material for the ... ?

3. Can you get the word order right?
on Monday and Tuesday – to the public – The fair – from 10 a.m. to 6 p.m. – will be open

Answer

1. application deadline
   catalogue of exhibitors
   stand rental
2. Please list us in the catalogue of exhibitors. How many complimentary tickets can we have? When do you need the promotional material for the press release?
3. The fair will be open to the public on Monday and Tuesday from 10 a.m. to 6 p.m.

business vocabulary:

press release – Pressemitteilung
promotional material – Werbematerial

Question

1. Put in the present continuous of *to shrink, to close down, to drop, to reduce.* They ... branch factories and ... workforce in order to become more competitive. The price of software ... and the profits of the big software houses ... .
2. Choose the right word. Our company has launched a new promotional *action / campaign* in France. They took legal *action / campaign* against a competitor who used one of their brand names.
3. Make two present tense sentences. Use the fitting verb forms!
   demand – for oil – rise – while – supply – fall.
   prices – therefore – expect – rise.

Answer

1. They are closing down branch factories and are reducing workforce in order to become more competitive. The price of software is dropping and the profits of the big software houses are shrinking.

2. Our company has launched a new promotional campaign in France. They took legal action against a competitor who used one of their brand names.
3. Demand for oil is rising while supply is falling. The prices therefore are expected to rise.

business vocabulary:

branch factory – Zweigfabrik
brand name – Markenname

Question

1. Preparing a business trip: Put in the fitting verb forms. "Ms. Maier (to arrive) on December 2nd on flight No. LH 803. Could you please (to arrange) for her (to pick up) from the airport?" "She (to meet) by Ms. Watkins. We are looking forward (to get to know) Ms. Maier."

2. Fixing a date. Make a short dialogue.
   - fix – date – visit of Mr. Jones.
   - June 3rd – suitable – Mr. Jones?
   - afraid – won't go. – What about – 4th?
   - 4th – just as good.

3. Can you get the word order right? force him – until March 21st – in Mr. Jones' scheduling – to postpone – Unforeseen difficulties – his visit.

Answer

1. will arrive – arrange – to be picked up – will be met – to getting to know
2. "I would like to fix a date for the visit of Mr. Jones."
   "Would June 3rd be suitable for Mr. Jones?"
   "I'm afraid, that won't go. What about the 4th?"
   "The 4th would be just as good."
3. Unforeseen difficulties in Mr. Jones' scheduling force him to postpone his visit until March 21st.

business vocabulary:
to schedule – Zeitplan erstellen

Question

1. Complete the following dialogue. Use the fitting forms of *to offer, to take, to be.*
   "Please ... a seat. Can I ... you something to drink?"
   "A glass of water ... very nice."
   "There you ... ."

2. Which answer doesn't fit?
   "Could you send me your brochure, please?“
   - "Certainly."
   - "Don't mention it."
   - "Yes, of course."

3. What are these public holidays called in English?
   - Ostern
   - Erster Weihnachtsfeiertag
   - Silvester

Answer

1. "Please take a seat. Can I offer you something to drink?"
   "A glass of water would be very nice."
   "There you are."
2. "Don't mention it."
3. • Easter
   • Christmas Day
   • New Year's Eve

Question

1. Choose the fitting verbs.
If you *require* / *demand* any further information, please do not *expect* / *hesitate* to contact us.

2. Complete this part of a business letter.
which we received - to be returned - look forward to - with reference to - Unfortunately - could send us - arranging
I am writing ... a delivery of 25 robot dogs ... on Friday, 11/6. ... four of them do not work. I am therefore ... for them ... to you. I would be grateful if you ... four new ones as soon as possible. I ... hearing from you.

3. What do these abbreviations stand for?
c/o • encl. • re(f).

Answer

1. If you require any further information, please do not hesitate to contact us.

2. I am writing with reference to a delivery of 25 robot dogs which we received on Friday, 11/6. Unfortunately four of them do not work. I am therefore arranging for them to be returned to you. I would be grateful if you could send us four new ones as soon as possible. I look forward to hearing from you.
3. • care of (dt. bei)
   • enclosed (dt. anbei)
   • with reference to (dt. betrifft)

business vocabulary:

to return – zurückschicken, -geben
to arrange for s.th. – für etwas sorgen

Answer

1. I have worked in the advertising sector for over ten years. I spent three years with Collins & Tomlinson. Then I moved on to Jones & Co. There my work included presenting catalogues, giving demonstrations to customers and carrying out advertising campaigns.

2. • copies of certificates and diplomas
   • a curriculum vitae

3. I have a written and spoken command of French, English and German.

business vocabulary:
curriculum vitae (CV) - Lebenslauf

Question

1. Applying for a job. Complete the sentences.
   carrying out – have worked – demonstrations to customers – spent – included – for over ten years – moved on
   I ... in the advertising sector ... . I ... three years with Collins & Tomlinson. Then I ... to Jones & Co. There my work ... presenting catalogues, giving ... and ... advertising campaigns.
2. What do you usually enclose in your application?
   - copies of certificates and diplomas
   - pictures of your family
   - a curriculum vitae

3. Can you get the word order right?
   and spoken command – I have – of French, English and German – a written

Answer

1. He's an expert in the development of business software.
   We have considerable expertise in developing high technology equipment.
2. She was elected entrepreneur of the year 2000.
3. • EDV-Branche
   • Pharma-Industrie
   • Krankenversicherungsgesellschaft
   • Baufirma

business vocabulary:

entrepreneur – Unternehmer
undertaker – Leichenbestatter
expertise – Fachkenntnis

Question

1. Complete the sentences using *expertise* or *expert*.
   He's an ... in the development of business software.
   We have considerable ... in developing high technology equipment.
2. Choose the right word.
   She was elected *undertaker/entrepreneur* of the year 2000.
3. Which is the German word for ...
   ... DP industry?
   ... pharmaceutical industry?
   ... medical insurance company?
   ... construction company?

Answer

1. I would like to add an item to the agenda. I haven't got the minutes of our last meeting.
2. Neujahr
   Karfreitag
   Heiligabend

3. There are two decisions to be taken.
   There are several issues to be discussed.
   There are two problems to be solved (auch: to be discussed).

business vocabulary:
minutes – Protokoll

Question

1. Choose the fitting words.
I would like to add an item to the *calendar / agenda.*
I haven't got the *seconds / minutes* of our last meeting.

2. What are these public holidays called in German?
   - New Year's Day
   - Good Friday
   - Christmas Eve

3. Match up the sentences.

There are two decisions	to be solved.
There are several issues	to be taken.
There are two problems	to be discussed.

Question

1. What are these cities called in English?
Den Haag • Athen • Genf • Wien

2. At the airport: passport control. Answer the questions.
"What's your nationality?"
- (German)
"What's the purpose of your visit?"
- (business)
"How long are you planning to stay?"
- (three days)

3. What are the German words for
... baggage claim?
... baggage rack?
... baggage trolley?
... baggage check-in?

Answer

1. The Hague • Athens • Geneva • Vienna

2. I'm German.
   I'm here on business.
   I'm going to stay for three days.
3. Gepäckausgabe
   Gepäckablage
   Gepäckwagen
   Gepäckabfertigung

Question

1. Choose the fitting word.
   My *chef / boss* Ms. Watkins is a highly qualified woman.
   There is a new *chef / boss* at the Le Canard restaurant.

2. Can you get the word order right?
   very much – thank you all – for your hospitality – We wish to

3. What are the German equivalents for
   ... last night?
   ... tonight?
   ... tomorrow night?

Answer

1. My boss Ms. Watkins is a highly qualified woman.
   There is a new chef at the Le Canard restaurant.

2. We wish to thank you all very much for your hospitality.
3. gestern Abend
   heute Abend
   morgen Abend

business vocabulary:
hospitality – Gastfreundschaft

Question

1. Complete the sentence using the fitting form of *to grow*.
   By the time I sold off the shares my investment ... by 65%.

2. Choose the fitting verb.
   She has *saved / spared* enough money to set up her own business.
   By taking in a partner she *saved / spared* herself a lot of trouble.

3. Can you match up the phrases?

to do	a profit
to make	at a loss
to sell	business with

Answer

1. By the time I sold off the shares my investment had grown by 65 %.

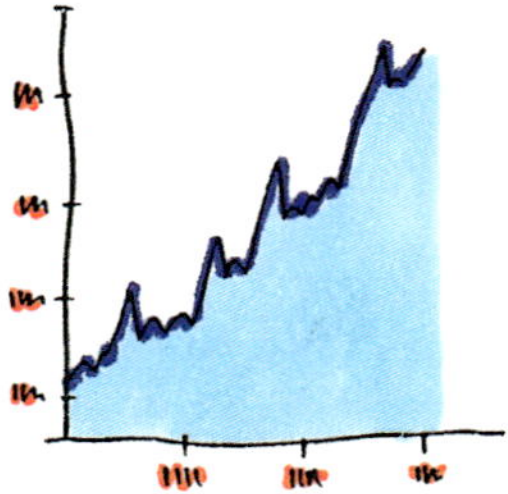

2. She has saved enough money to set up her own business.
   By taking in a partner she spared herself a lot of trouble.

3. to do business with
   to make a profit
   to sell at a loss

Question

1. *for* or *in*?
   He handed in an application ... the job of an advertising manager.
   He has a lot of experience ... all kinds of promotional campaigns.
   The company seems to be interested ... taking him on.

2. Complete the sentence.
   I am familiar with operating

   the  and the 

3. Make sentences using *has / have been*.
   - vacancy – already – fill
   - position – already – take over – by somebody else

Answer

1. He handed in an application for the job of an advertising manager.
   He has a lot of experience in all kinds of promotional campaigns.
   The company seems to be interested in taking him on.
2. I am familiar with operating the fax machine and the PC.
3. The vacancy has already been filled.
   The position has already been taken over by somebody else.

Question

1. *of* or *to*?
   to transfer ...
   to consist ...
   to respond ...
2. Put in *must* plus the fitting forms of *to pay* and *to make*.
   All invoices ... without any deduction or added fees.
   Payment ... in French currency by transfer to one of the bank accounts stated in the invoice.

3. Choose the fitting words.
   Please find *enclosed / inlying* the *invoice / bill* in triplicate. The *terms / trends* of payment are 14 days net.

Answer

1. to transfer to
   to consist of
   to respond to
2. All invoices must be paid without any deduction or added fees. Payment must be made in French currency by transfer to one of the bank accounts stated in the invoice.

3. enclosed
   invoice
   terms

business vocabulary:
deduction – Abzug

Question

1. *discount, provision* or *condition*?
You get a generous ... when ordering more than twenty tricycles.

2. Choose the fitting word.
Our company is moving to new *premises / promises.*

3. Match up the phrases.

to be famous	to
to be accustomed	of
to be aware	with
to be satisfied	for

Answer

1. You get a generous discount when ordering more than twenty tricycles.

2. Our company is moving to new premises.
3. to be famous for
   to be accustomed to
   to be aware of
   to be satisfied with

business vocabulary:
premises – Räumlichkeiten

Question

1. Make two sentences.
   I - meeting - moment. - I - call - back?
2. *Do you call* or *Are you calling*?
   The line is very bad. ... from your mobile phone?

3. Complete the dialogue.
   Hold on - to speak to - this is - the line's busy - call back later - help you - like to
   "Manchester Toys Limited, good morning. Can I ... ?"
   "Hello, ... Sandra Maier. I'd like ... Ms. Watkins, please."
   "... , please. - I'm afraid ... . Would you ... hold?"
   "It's all right, thanks. I'll ... ."

Answer

1. I'm in a meeting at the moment. Can I call you back?
2. The line is very bad. Are you calling from your mobile phone?

3. "Manchester Toys Limited, good morning. Can I help you?" "Hello, this is Sandra Maier. I'd like to speak to Ms. Watkins, please." "Hold on, please. – I'm afraid the line's busy. Would you like to hold?" "It's all right, thanks. I'll call back later."

telephone vocabulary:

busy – besetzt
to hold (on) – am Apparat bleiben
line – Leitung
mobile phone – Handy

Question

1. Booking a room. Choose the fitting phrases.
   I'd like to *book / reserve* two single rooms with bath for the nights of September 2nd to 4th. I'm *non-smoker / a non-smoker*. How much is that *for the night / per night*? I'll *conform / confirm* my booking by fax.
2. Write a confirmation for the above booking.

3. What are the German expressions for ...
   ... bed and breakfast?
   ... double room?
   ... no vacancies?

Answer

1. I'd like to book two single rooms with bath for the nights of September 2nd to 4th. I'm a non-smoker. How much is that per night? I'll confirm my booking by fax.
2. This is to confirm our telephone conversation of ... in which I booked two single non-smoking rooms for the nights of September 2nd to 4th.
3. Übernachtung mit Frühstück
   Doppelzimmer
   ausgebucht

Question

1. Put in *is / are* and the *-ing* form.
   Interest rates ... (still / to rise) and the economy ... (to slow down).
2. What are the German words for ...
   ... retailer?
   ... wholesaler?
3. Complete the sentences.
   has sold – the export rate – we are hoping – relaxed – last year
   Since the Chinese government ... export regulations ..., our company ... a lot of bicycles to China. And next year ... to increase ... further.

Answer

1. Interest rates are still rising and the economy is slowing down.
2. Einzelhändler
   Großhändler
3. Since the Chinese government relaxed export regulations last year, our company has sold a lot of bicycles to China. And next year we are hoping to increase the export rate further.

Question

1. Sort these letter endings on a scale from very formal to informal.
   Yours sincerely • Yours • With best regards • Yours faithfully
2. Can you get the word order right?
   wooden play figures - samples - are pleased - of our brand new - We - to submit

3. Make polite sentenses.
   send us - list - products - manufacture. - we - keep - goods - on a trial basis - one month?

Answer

1. • Yours faithfully
   • Yours sincerely
   • With best regards
   • Yours
2. We are pleased to submit samples of our brand new wooden play figures.

3. Please send us a list of the products you manufacture.
   Could we keep the goods on a trial basis for one month?

business vocabulary:

on a trial basis – zur Probe
to submit samples – Muster vorlegen

Question

1. What are the German equivalents for ...
   ... the day before yesterday?
   ... the day after tomorrow?
   ... a week on Thursday?
2. Make new sentences using *to have something done.*
   He washed his car yesterday.
   She is going to install a new PC.

3. "I beg your pardon." Which response doesn't fit?
   - "That's OK."
   - "Don't mention it."
   - "What a pity!"

Answer

1. vorgestern
   übermorgen
   Donnerstag in einer Woche
2. He had his car washed yesterday.
   She's going to have a new PC installed.
3. "What a pity!"

Question

1. What are they called in English?

2. Hotel services: Ask polite questions.
   - when – breakfast?
   - order –

   - accept – credit cards?
   - get ready – bill?

3. Which phrase is right?
   Is there a *money automat / cash dispenser* near the hotel?

Answer

1. TV
   alarm clock
2. • When is breakfast served, please?
   • Could you please order a taxi for me?
   • Do you accept credit cards?
   • Could you please get my bill ready?
3. Is there a cash dispenser near the hotel?

Question

1. Complete the sentences using the fitting forms of *to win / to sign*.
   They are quite relieved to ... the contract.
   They ... (already) the deal.

2. Make two sentences.
   design – new car – finished – last month. –
   They – already – build – prototype.

3. Can you match up the phrases?

to go	a meeting
to pay	bankrupt
to have	in advance

Answer

1. They are quite relieved to have won the contract.
   They have already signed the deal.
2. The design for the new car was finished last month. They are already building a prototype.

3. to go bankrupt
   to pay in advance
   to have a meeting

business vocabulary:
contract – Vertrag

Question

1. Can you get the word order right?
as a safety inspector – May I – my services – offer
are suitable – My experience – for the position – and qualifications
2. "Basic knowledge of data-processing is mandatory." What does *mandatory* mean?
   - optional
   - compulsory
   - needless
3. Complete the sentences.
in order to fix – your application – call you – we inform you
Herewith ... that ... has been retained.
We will ... within the next few days ... an interview.

Answer

1. May I offer my services as a safety inspector?

My experience and qualifications are suitable for the position.

2. compulsory

3. Herewith we inform you that your application has been retained. We will call you within the next few days in order to fix an interview.

business vocabulary:

to retain – behalten

Question

1. Choose the right words.
We wish to inform you that the *goods / wares* you ordered last week will be *dispersed / dispatched* tomorrow.

2. Complete the sentences.
In order - the whole shipment - in time for the - air freight - for the delay
We are very sorry ... in delivery. ... that you have the merchandise ... Christmas period, we sent ... today via ... .

3. What is the German word for ...
... importing firm?
... distribution company?
... trading company?

Answer

1. We wish to inform you that the goods you ordered last week will be dispatched tomorrow.

2. We are very sorry for the delay in delivery. In order that you have the merchandise in time for the Christmas period, we sent the whole shipment today via air freight.

3. Importfirma
   Vertriebsgesellschaft
   Handelsgesellschaft

business vocabulary:

to dispatch – losschicken, expedieren
to disperse – verstreuen
shipment – Lieferung

Question

1. Choose the fitting word.
   Most MTL products are available at all the major German *warehouses / department stores.*

2. What are these words in German?
   - decade
   - century
   - millennium
3. Can you say it a bit more politely?
   - Give me a cup of tea.
   - What do you want?

Answer

1. Most MTL products are available at all the major German department stores.
2. Jahrzehnt
   Jahrhundert
   Jahrtausend

3. Possible sentences:
   - Can I have a cup of tea?
   - What can I do for you?

business vocabulary:
warehouse – Warenlager, Lagerhaus

Question

1. Say the telephone number *649937*.
2. Choose the fitting verb.
   May I ask who I'm *talking / speaking* to?

3. Complete the dialogue.
   code is – I take – ask him – in a meeting – your number – your message

   "I'm afraid, Mr. Butler is ... . Can I ... a message?"
   "Could you ... to call me back?"
   "What's ... , please?"
   "It's 5480033. The ... 004940."
   "All right. I'll give him ... ."

Answer

1. six four double nine three seven
2. May I ask who I'm speaking to?

3. in a meeting – I take – ask him – your number – The code is – your message

telephone vocabulary:
code – Vorwahl

Question

1. Ask your way around. Make questions.
   - when – next train – Brighton?
   - platform – leave?
   - how long – take?
   - where – bus stop?
   - where – ticket for the underground?
2. Complete the sentence using the present tense of *to arrive, to stop* and *to be.*
   There ... a train tomorrow at 1.35. It ... in Liverpool at 4.16 and it ... on the way only twice.
3. What are they called in English?

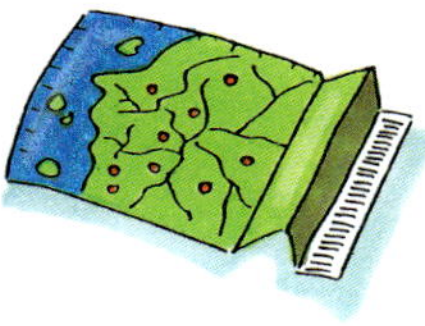

Answer

1. Possible questions are:
   When's the next train to Brighton?
   Which platform does it leave from?
   How long does it take?
   Where's the bus stop, please?
   Where can I buy a ticket for the underground, please?

2. There is a train tomorrow at 1.35. It arrives in Liverpool at 4.16 and it stops on the way only twice.

3. map
   driving license

Question

1. Choose the right word.
A company which produces lipsticks is in the *cosmologic / cosmetic* industry.
A wholesaler of food is in the *grocer / grocery* business.

A firm which produces hair dryers is in the *electrical / electronic* industry.

2. Make new sentences using *to have something done.*
We print our books in Singapore.
They manufacture their cars in Hungary.

3. Choose the fitting word.
Our *headquarters / centres* are in Frankfurt, but we have *branch / brunch* offices in Stuttgart and Leipzig.

! Answer

1. A company which produces lipsticks is in the cosmetic industry.
   A wholesaler of food is in the grocery business.
   A firm which produces hair dryers is in the electrical industry.
2. We have our books printed in Singapore. They have their cars manufactured in Hungary.

3. Our headquarters are in Frankfurt, but we have branch offices in Stuttgart and Leipzig.

Question

1. Complete the following speech.
great pleasure – On behalf of – speak to you – German toy market – to welcome
... Manchester Toys Limited I'd like ... you all. I have ... to introduce Ms. Sandra Maier from German Toys who will now ... about special features of the ... .

2. Make a polite sentence.
I – have – attention?

3. Choose the fitting verb.
I *admire / appreciate* that you are *spending / sacrificing* some of your valuable time.

Answer

1. On behalf of Manchester Toys Limited I'd like to welcome you all. I have great pleasure to introduce Ms. Sandra Maier from German Toys who will now speak to you about special features of the German toy market.

2. Could I / May I have your attention, please?

3. I appreciate that you are sacrificing some of your valuable time.

Question

1. Renting a car. Make a dialogue.
   - how much – daily rental – Ford Fiesta
   - offer you – special rate – three days, mileage included
   - what – insurance – cover
   - third party insurance
   - leave – car – airport?
   - of course

2. What are the German words for ...
   ... automatic transmission?
   ... manual gear change?
3. At the petrol station. You've run out of petrol. What do you say?
   - "Recharge it."
   - "Adjust it."
   - "Fill it up."

Answer

1. • "How much is the daily rental for a Ford Fiesta?"
   • "We can offer you a special rate for three days, mileage included."
   • "What does the insurance cover?"
   • "It's a third party insurance."
   • "Can I leave the car at the airport?"
   • "Yes, of course."
2. • Automatikgetriebe
   • Schaltgetriebe
3. "Fill it up."

Car vocabulary:

third party insurance – Haftpflichtversicherung
comprehensive insurance – Vollkaskoversicherung
unlimited mileage – unbegrenzte Kilometerzahl

Question

1. Choose the fitting words.
We would ask you to inform us why *payment / shipment* of our invoice No. 111 *amounting / mounting* to 150.00 Euro has not yet been *effected / effaced.*

2. What is the German word for *reminder*?

3. Which of the sentences sounds wrong?
   - Payment of our invoice No. 111 is now eight weeks overdue.
   - We still have not received your remittance for our invoice No. 111.
   - You did not pay invoice No. 111 yet.

Answer

1. We would ask you to inform us why payment of our invoice No. 111 amounting to 150.00 Euro has not yet been effected.
2. Mahnung

3. You did not pay invoice No. 111 yet.

Question

1. Which noun does not fit?
   information
   equipment
   advice
   horse

2. A business meeting. Complete the sentences.
   of the agenda – coming here – received – on behalf of the management
   Ladies and Gentlemen, ... I would like to thank you for ... today. Has everyone ... a copy ...?
3. You want to sum up the points discussed. Do you *summarise* or *add up*?

Answer

1.

2. Ladies and Gentlemen, on behalf of the management I would like to thank you for coming here today. Has everyone received a copy of the agenda?

3. summarise

business vocabulary:

agenda – Tagesordnung
equipment – Anlage, Maschine, Ausrüstung

Question

1. On the phone: Can you say it a bit more politely?
   - What's your name?
   - Call back later!
   - What did you say?
2. Complete the sentences using *in* and *on*.
   - Who's ... the phone?
   - I'm afraid I'm ... a hurry.
   - Who's ... charge of today's delivery of rocking horses to Hamburg?

3. Say the telephone number *547773*.

Answer

1. Possible sentences:
   May I ask who is calling?
   Could you call back later?
   Could you repeat that?

2. • Who's on the phone?
   • I'm afraid I'm in a hurry.
   • Who's in charge of today's delivery of rocking horses to Hamburg?
3. five four seven double seven three

POCKET QUIZ
Business Englisch
150 Fragen und Antworten
moses.

2. Auflage 2007

moses. Verlag GmbH
Arnoldstraße 13d
47906 Kempen
Fon 0 21 52 – 20 98 50
Fax 0 21 52 – 20 98 60
Mail info@moses-verlag.de
www.moses-verlag.de

ISBN 978-3-89777-052-2

Text: Dr. Anne Emmert
Illustrationen: Bianca Peters

Printed in Germany

Question

1. At the exchange office. Make sentences.
   - change – 200 Euros – pounds.
   - rate – today?
   - receipt?

2. Which verbs fit?
   You can *cash / balance* a cheque.
   You can *transfer / translate* money to another account.
   You can *withdraw / withhold* money from your account.

3. At the bank. Can you match the sentences?

I'd like to change

do you charge?

I'd like to cash

700 Euros into pounds.

What commission

this traveller cheque.

Answer

1. Possible sentences:
   - I'd like to change 200 Euros into pounds, please.
   - What's the rate today?
   - Could I have a receipt, please?
2. • cash • transfer • withdraw

3. I'd like to change 700 Euros into pounds.
   I'd like to cash this traveller cheque.
   What commission do you charge?

bank vocabulary:

account – Konto
commission – Bankgebühr
to draw / withdraw – abheben
rate – Wechselkurs
receipt – Quittung

Answer

1. "Excuse me, could you spare me a minute?"
   "Certainly. What can I do for you?"
   "I'm interested in the technical details of this device."
   "You'll find everything in this brochure. By the way, you get our products at the trade fair discount of 20 %."

2. to be interested in
   to apply for
   to take part in
3. I can offer you a couple of products that would meet your requirements.

business vocabulary:

booth – Messestand

Question

1. Trade fair: at the booth. Complete the dialogue.
   at the trade fair discount - spare me - in this brochure - do for you - interested in

   "Excuse me, could you ... a minute?"
   "Certainly. What can I ... ?"
   "I'm ... the technical details of this device."
   "You'll find everything ... . By the way, you get our products ... of 20 %."

2. *in* or *for*?
   to be interested ...
   to apply ...
   to take part ...

3. Can you get the word order right?
   a couple of - your requirements - that - I can offer you - products - would meet

Question

1. Choose the right word.
Because of training courses and my *day-time / everyday* work with a PC, I have *acquired / received* a thorough knowledge of all business-related programmes.

2. Complete the following advert.
salary proposals – by June 8th – the following address – are seeking – enclosing
We ... an experienced sales manageress ... . Please send applications ... a curriculum vitae and including ... to ... .

3. What don't you mention in your curriculum vitae?
   - education
   - your friends and favourite pubs
   - courses and seminars
   - previous jobs

Answer

1. Because of training courses and every-day work with a PC, I have acquired a thorough knowledge of all business-related programmes.
2. We are seeking an experienced sales manageress by June 8th. Please send applications enclosing a curriculum vitae and including salary proposals to the following address.
3. your friends and favourite pubs